Money Around the W

Using Money

Rebecca Rissman

Heinemann Library
Chicago, Illinois

www.heinemannraintree.com
Visit our website to find out
more information about
Heinemann-Raintree books.

To order:

☎ Phone 888-454-2279

💻 Visit www.heinemannraintree.com
to browse our catalog and order online.

Edited by Rebecca Rissman, Siân Smith, and Charlotte Guillain
Designed by Kimberly Miracle and Joanna Malivoire
Picture research by Tracy Cummins
Originated by Capstone Global Library
Printed and bound in China by Leo Paper Products Ltd

13 12 11 10 09
10 9 8 7 6 5 4 3 2 1

Library of Congress Cataloging-in-Publication Data
Rissman, Rebecca.
  Using money / Rebecca Rissman.
       p. cm.
  Includes bibliographical references and index.
  ISBN 978-1-4329-3265-7 (hc)
  ISBN 978-1-4329-3266-4 (pb)
  1. Money--Juvenile literature. I. Title.
  HG222.5.R57 2009
  332.4--dc22
                      2008055317

Acknowledgments

The author and publishers are grateful to the following for
permission to reproduce copyright material: Age Fotostock p.**20**
(© Flying Colours Ltd); Alamy p.**9** (© JLImages); Getty Images
pp.**4** (© Lifesize/Brand New Images), **5 right** (© Taxi/Zubin
Shroff), **7** (© The Image Bank/Livia Corona), **8** (© Iconica/
Andersen Ross), **10** (© Purestock), **15** (© Keith Brofsky), **16 left**
(© Photodisc/Alberto Coto), **17** (© Salah Malkawi), **18** (© Gallo
Images/Shaen Adey), **19** (© Photographer's Choice/Hugh Sitton),
21 right (© Nick Dolding); Photolibrary pp.**6** (© Blend Images RF/
DreamPictures/Pam Ostrow), **11** (© Digital Vision/PNC PNC),
16 middle (© Index Stock Imagery/Barry Winiker), **16 right** (©
Blend Images RF/Ariel Skelley), **22 left** (© Digital Vision/PNC
PNC), **22 right** (© Radius Images); Shutterstock pp.**5 left** (© David
Gilder), **12** (© Lena Bernatsky), **13** (© Vincent Giordano), **14** (©
Tischenko Irina); The World Bank p.**21 left** (© Eric Miller).

Front cover photograph reproduced with permission of age
fotostock (© Michel Renaudeau). Back cover photograph
reproduced with permission of Getty Images (© Lifesize/Brand
New Images).

We would like to thank Nancy Harris and Adriana Scalise for
their help in the preparation of this book.

Every effort has been made to contact copyright holders of
any material reproduced in this book. Any omissions will
be rectified in subsequent printings if notice is given to the
publisher.

Some words are shown in bold, **like this.** They are
explained in "Words to Know" on page 23.

Contents

What Is Money? 4

Wants and Needs 8

Different Types of Money. 12

Getting Money 16

Saving Money 20

A Want or A Need? 22

Words to Know 23

Index 24

Note to Parents and Teachers 24

About this series

Books in the **Money Around the World** series introduce children to the concepts of currency, exchange, and global diversity. Use this book to stimulate discussion about how and why money is used.

What Is Money?

Money is something we use to **trade**. We give people money to get things.

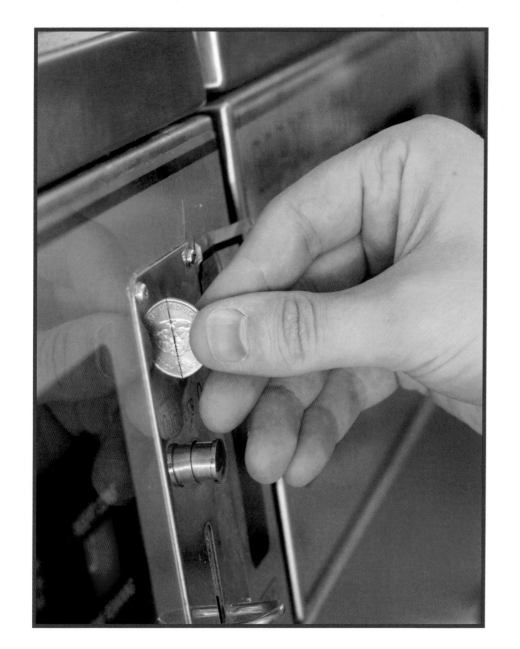 

We **exchange** money for things. There are different types of money.

Money can be used to buy things. We **spend** money to buy things.

We can sell things for money. We **earn** money when we sell things.

Wants and Needs

We use money when we need things. We **spend** money on things we need.

Needs are things that we must have in order to live. We must have food, water, and shelter.

We use money when we want things. We **spend** money on things we want.

Wants are things that we do not need in order to live. Toys, music, and jewelry are wants.

Different Types of Money

People use different types of money. Coins are small, round pieces of metal. Coins are money. Different countries may use different coins.

Bills are rectangles of paper. Bills are money.
Different countries may use different bills.

Credit cards and **debit cards** are small pieces of plastic. Credit cards and debit cards can be used like money. Different countries may use different types of credit cards and debit cards.

Checks are pieces of paper that people write on. Checks can be used like money. Different countries may use different types of checks.

Getting Money

People work to **earn** money. People work at different jobs.

People are paid money to work at jobs. People are given **paychecks** for work.

Some people work selling **goods** to **earn** money. Goods are things we eat or use.

Some people work selling **services** to earn money.
Services are jobs people do for others.

Saving Money

People can save money for later. Saving money means not **spending** it. Saving money means putting it somewhere safe.

People can save money in banks. People can save money in jars. People can save money to buy something special!

A Want or A Need?

Which picture shows a **want**?
Which picture shows a **need**?

Answer on page 24.

Words to Know

check   paper that people write on and use like money

credit card   plastic card used like money

debit card   plastic card used like money

earn   to get money for work you have done

exchange   swap

goods   things we eat or use

needs   what people must have. Food, clothing, and housing are needs.

paycheck   a check that people get for work they have done

service   a job people do for others

spend   to use money to get something

trade   to give something in order to get something else

wants   what people do not need. We do not need toys, vacations, or TVs but we do want them.

Index

bill 5, 13
card 14, 23
check 15, 23
coin 5, 12

goods 18, 23
needs 9, 22, 23
save 20, 21
sell 7, 18, 19

service 19, 23
wants 11, 22, 23
work 16, 17, 18, 19

Note to Parents and Teachers

Before reading

Ask children if they know what money is. How do people get money? After children respond, tell them that money is something we use to trade to get things we need or want. People earn money by working or selling things. Ask children if they have ever earned money. Tell children that there are different types of money. People can also use plastic credit cards or paper checks when they need to pay for things. Ask children if they have ever seen a credit card or check.

After reading

• Discuss the difference between selling goods and selling services. Make a list with children of different ways people can earn money. As the list is being created, ask if each job relates to goods or services.

• Set up a role-play area as a work place such as a grocery store with cashiers, baggers, managers, delivery people, and shoppers. Encourage the children to play in role and to use play money to pay for goods and services.

Answer to question on page 22

The picture showing someone looking at jewelry shows a want.

The picture of someone buying food shows a need.